STEAMERS of the FORTH
Volume 2: Firth Services and Excursions
by
Ian Brodie

Dating from 1886, *Fair Maid* was acquired by the Grangemouth & Forth Towing Co. in 1927 to operate excursions. She also acted as a tender to visiting cruise liners, and as the relief vessel for the London & North Eastern Railway's Queensferry (until 1933) and Burntisland crossings. When tendering she operated from this passenger terminal on the east side of the Water of Leith.

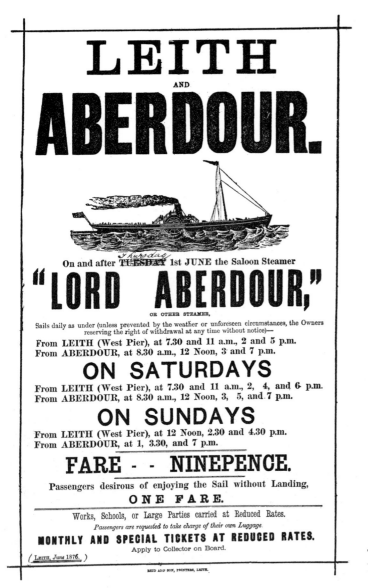

© Ian Brodie 2004
First published in the United Kingdom, 2004,
by Stenlake Publishing Ltd.
Telephone: 01290 551122
Printed by Cordfall Ltd. Glasgow, G21 2QA

ISBN 1 84033 308 1

The publishers regret that they cannot supply copies of any pictures featured in this book.

PICTURE CREDITS

Alan Brotchie: p9, p21 (lower), p31 (upper), p48 (upper), back cover; Douglas Brown: p12 (both), p31 (lower), p38 (upper), p43; Dundee Public Libraries, Local Studies Department: p13; Eric Eunson: p10 (both), p28 (upper); Ian Quinn: p11, p41; Douglas Yuill: p3, p27, p30 (both), p35 (upper), p37, p39.

This poster for the Leith and Aberdour passage was originally used during the 1875 season, and the date was subsequently altered to 1876.

INTRODUCTION

Together with a companion volume subtitled 'Ferry Crossings and River Sailings', this book tells the story of local passenger sailings on the River and Firth of Forth. All activity relating to services starting east of the Queensferry narrows is covered in this volume, with the exception of the Fife and Midlothian ferries from Newhaven to Pettycur and Burntisland, and their successor between Granton and Burntisland, which were controlled by Parliamentary Act and feature in volume one.

The relatively high speeds attainable by steam-powered vessels, and their ability to operate regardless of wind conditions, opened up myriad opportunities for entrepreneurs wishing to transport goods and passengers along river and coastal routes from the 1820s onwards. Journeys by water were often substantially shorter than routes via land, and there was a ready market for the steamer services, both from passenger and goods traffic. A secondary and generally seasonal excursion trade became increasingly lucrative, providing a variety of day trips during summer months. This had the added benefit of providing part-time work for steamers which might otherwise be idle due to unfavourable tidal conditions.

Most traffic on the Forth originated from the Edinburgh area, and piers and harbours were built close to the city to handle this. Early sailings served Fife, mostly to the east of the parliamentary ferry routes, though an embryonic Aberdour passage was operational by the 1850s and encouraged the development of the village as a resort. At Portobello an elegant pier – in the English manner, with entertainments – opened in 1871. Although steamer calls were of secondary importance to the pier, a weekly service from Leith via Portobello flourished.

In the 1870s *Fiery Cross*, a small tug with a strong personality, became the Forth's favourite focus for day trips. Three generations of the Galloway family were involved in the firth's

major excursion enterprise, the Galloway Saloon Steam Packet Co. These were Captain John Galloway (on early Aberdour services); his son Matthew, who managed a pleasure fleet of six 'yachts' from his Leith ship chandler's and engineering business; and his son John, who took over the running of the company just before the First World War. That conflict saw the sailings come to an end, and the company's piers either became derelict or were demolished afterwards. The Galloway chandlery business survived into the 1950s, with half-hull models of the steamers decorating its staircase.

As the twentieth century progressed, an improved road network quickly eroded the commercial viability of steamer sailings as a means of travelling between towns, but the excursion trade continued. Local excursions in the 1920s and 30s were mostly provided by Grangemouth tug-owners and confined to the area upstream from Kirkcaldy and Portobello. Open-water excursions (those to the coast and beyond) were only available for three years in the 1920s, and a further three in the mid-1930s, using elderly steamers, all of which were soon destined to go to the shipbreakers.

The late 1940s saw a brief revival of the excursion trade with modern tonnage, and from 1977 a sludge ship provided free day cruises for small groups. Small launches have since provided services to the various islands of the Forth Estuary, and recently these have been upgraded, with two attractive small ships in operation during 2004. The Forth also enjoys brief visits from the preserved motor-ship *Balmoral*, providing opportunities for longer excursions.

A Galloway Co. steamer from Leith provided Sunday cruises from Kirkcaldy until the summer of 1907, after which the service was taken over by the Kirkcaldy Towing Co., using their tug *Fifeshire*, which maintained the excursions until 1914. On Fife holidays she cruised from Kirkcaldy to Aberdour, Rosyth dockyard or the Forth Bridge. She is seen here sharing the stone pier at Aberdour with Galloway's *Edinburgh Castle*.

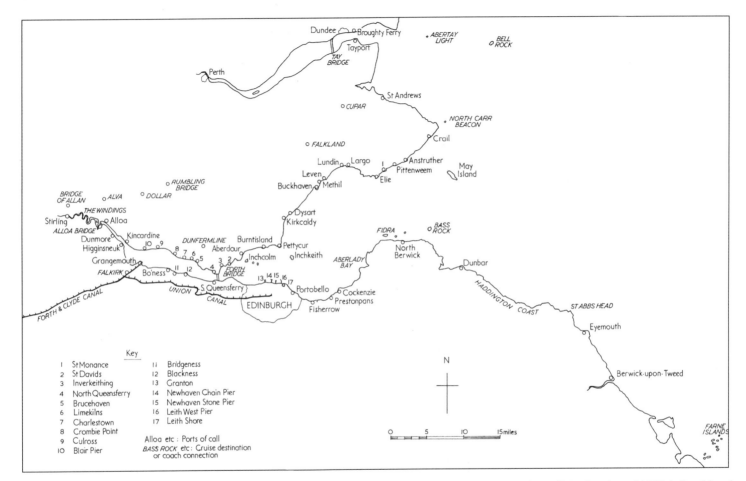

This map of the River and Firth of Forth shows all steamer ports of call and cruise destinations. The Merchant Shipping Act of 1855 defined local areas of operation for passenger shipping, as well as stipulating conditions of carriage including the space required per passenger and mandatory lifesaving equipment. Vessels were issued with certificates detailing the number of passengers permitted based on the type of waters they were sailing in. For the Forth, calm water was specified as above the Queensferry narrows (steam five), and moderately calm water inside a line drawn from Portobello to Kirkcaldy (steam four). East of this a steam three certificate was required for daylight summertime sailing. A steam two home trade certificate was required for winter operation. More recently other certificates have been introduced, with a class six, for instance, allowing daylight operation within a specified distance of the coast.

This engraving shows the Edinburgh shore, with the Newhaven Chain Pier prominent in the foreground and the Stone Pier in the middle distance. Until a sandbar was dredged and the West Pier opened there in 1852, Leith was an unsuitable departure point for scheduled services, although many vessels loaded cargo there, entering at high tide and anchoring off Newhaven until sailing time. At low water passengers embarking at Newhaven were loaded by small boat, a practice known as 'florrying', until 1821 when the single-berth Chain Pier was opened, providing a low-water landing. For twenty years this was the focal point of the Forth services, remaining so until the Duke of Buccleuch opened his harbour at Granton in 1838, at which point most services migrated there, moving to Leith after the opening of the West Pier.

Managed by Andrew Greig, and purchased by him in 1840, the Chain Pier at Newhaven was thereafter used mainly by his own steamers. Once its days as a steamer terminal were over it was turned into a sea-bathing station and gymnasium until destroyed by a gale in 1898. Firth passenger services started in 1821 on the back of *Tourist*'s pioneering sailings to Aberdeen and London. Initially advertised by the Leith & Aberdeen Steam Yacht Company, *Tourist* was soon transferred to the London & Edinburgh Steam Packet Co., and on 4 July 1822 gave an excursion round the Bass Rock, May Island (landing) and Bell and Carr Rocks. As late as the 1850s steamers bound for Aberdeen stopped to florry passengers and goods at the East Neuk ports of

Elie, Anstruther and Crail, but passing calls were unsatisfactory for loading cargo and the East Neuk got a dedicated service in 1844, operated by the old *Stirling Castle*, owned by the Anstruther & Leith Steam Shipping Co. A new vessel, *Xantho*, was built in 1848, being replaced by *Forth* (not to be confused with the Burntisland ferry of the same name) in 1856, a fine two-masted vessel. Summer tourists latterly provided most of the traffic on this route and the service was discontinued in May 1875 when *Forth* became a coal hulk at Granton. In 1829 the Alloa, Stirling & Kincardine Steamboat Co., rather than have its vessels anchored off Newhaven when the tide was unsuitable for upriver runs, started landing cruises (those on which passengers could disembark) to Inchkeith, Inchcolm or May Island, but these became much less frequent once the fords at Stirling were removed in the 1840s, making the river navigable for longer periods on each tide. The East Lothian and Berwickshire coasts were never so well-served as Fife, though on occasions the London and Hull steamers made calls at Dunbar, Eyemouth and Berwick. There were also excursions from Fisherrow in 1836, with connecting trains from St Leonard's, Edinburgh, along a branch of the horse-drawn Edinburgh & Dalkeith Railway.

The statutory requirement to maintain a ferry service from the Edinburgh shore to the Fife ports of Pettycur and Burntisland ceased on the opening of a new Burntisland to Granton crossing on 5 September 1844. Vessels on the original crossing had also served Kirkcaldy, and aggrieved at the potential loss of its ferry service, the town continued to license the steamers permitted to call there. Until June 1848, by which time it was connected by rail to Burntisland, the former ferries *Queen* and *Edinburgh Castle* continued to operate from Newhaven to Kirkcaldy. The licenses were then purchased by the Edinburgh & Dundee Steam Packet Co., and that summer *Fair Trader* started at

Largo from the Shore. Steamers do not often run into Largo Harbour, but on this occasion one of the Leith Fleet is a welcome visitor. A good Harbour might be made here at comparatively small cost.

Anstruther in the morning, calling at Pittenweem, Elie, Largo, Leven, Dysart and Kirkcaldy on her run to the Chain Pier. The company's Dundee steamers also made a ferry run from the Chain Pier to Aberdour and Kirkcaldy between their Dundee sailings. After that concern folded, the Fife coast service became seasonal, with Andrew Greig chartering *Rival* in 1849, *Helen Macgregor* and *Rob Roy* in 1850/1, and *Samson* in 1852. As the Chain Pier was by then unfit to handle heavy goods, the nearby Stone Pier was used for all cargo and cattle loading, although passengers still embarked at the Chain Pier. Greig retired at the end of the 1852 season, and the following year the service was contracted to Leith tug-owners Hall & Stoker, with the terminus changed to the West Pier at Leith and the ex-Clyde steamer *Royal Victoria* placed on the route to Kirkcaldy and Pittenweem. The railway contractors Anderson's took the licenses in 1854, using the former Burntisland boat *Maid of Leven* from a terminus at Largo. The service ceased on the opening of the Leven Railway on 3 July 1854, although by August Leith tug-owners MacGregor & Galloway had taken over, running *Goliath* as far as Largo. Their *Alma* was placed on the service in 1855, but abandoned it on 29 June, after which there were no further takers for Kirkcaldy's steamboat licenses. This postcard shows the excursion steamer *Stirling Castle* at Largo in the 1890s.

In 1848 Andrew Greig ran a sporadic excursion service to Aberdour using his Dundee steamers, and with chartered tonnage thereafter. A tug called *Lion* was used on an excursion service from Leith to Aberdour, St David's and Inverkeithing in 1852, but it was only with the formation of the partnership of Donald MacGregor, a Leith insurance broker and merchant, and Captain John Galloway, shipmaster, in 1854, that a regular summer service began between Leith and the inner Fife coast. They operated a fleet of tugs, one of which was employed on passenger work running from the West Pier at Leith. During their first season *Carrs* was sailing to Aberdour and Inverkeithing, with an afternoon cruise to Inchcolm; in subsequent years the service was concentrated on Aberdour, with frequent calls at Inchcolm and occasional excursions to Kirkcaldy. Vessels used were *Alma, Energy, Xantho, Pilot, Blue Bonnet, Goliath, Ruby, Robert Scott* and *Pearl*, all of which were tugs except *Xantho*. By 1858 fares had stabilised at 9*d*. cabin and 6*d*. steerage, with those passengers not landing paying only a single fare. This picture shows *Ruby* alongside the Inchgarvie caisson of the Forth Bridge, during its construction in the mid-1880s.

MacGregor and Galloway obtained a proper excursion vessel from Glasgow shipbuilders Aitken & Mansell for the 1866 season. *Lord Aberdour*, a compact saloon steamer, was 142 feet long and named after a local landowner who gave a site near Hawkcraig Point (Aberdour) for the construction of a wooden pier for the exclusive use of the Galloway steamers. Suitable for landing at all states of the tide, this was certainly in use by 1870 when all calls were at the 'new pier'. By 1872 traffic had reverted to the town's stone pier, with the wooden pier becoming the low-water landing. A condition of the pier lease was that it could not be used on Sundays, but a Sunday service was provided from 1870 with passengers being florried ashore to the stone pier at low water. John Galloway died in April 1869, after which Donald MacGregor became sole owner. *Pearl*, the last of the passenger tugs, was sold in 1876. Here, *Fiery Cross* leads *Lord Aberdour* out of Leith.

In 1869 an Act of Parliament was obtained by a private company to build a pier at the expanding resort of Portobello. Thomas Bouch designed the elegant cast-iron structure, which was 1,250 feet long and laid out in the English style with a saloon and entertainments. It opened on 23 May 1871 with a call by *Lord Aberdour* and a ninety minute cruise to Prestonpans, followed by lunch in the pier saloon. That summer cruises to Aberdour were given by *Pearl* on Saturdays, but were not continued in future years. Thursday sailings by tug from Leith had started in 1866 with *Powerful* running to North Berwick and the May Island, and from 1870 a call at Portobello was added. *William Scott* and *Integrity* became the regular vessels on this route from 1872.

George Jamieson commenced Sunday sailings from Leith in 1867 using his tug *Garibaldi* as a floating drinking palace. The destination was Aberdour, where passengers were florried ashore, while Saturday trips were also given to May Island with three hours ashore. *Garibaldi* was sunk while towing off North Berwick in June 1870, and the Sunday service was restarted by *Fiery Cross* in 1872, operating to Burntisland and Kirkcaldy. In 1874 she also took over the established Thursday run to North Berwick and Bass Rock, soon extended to May Island. Aberdour became the Sunday destination in 1876 in an atmosphere of intense competition, culminating in a fight on the West Pier at Leith on 27 August leading to Jamieson being fined 20s. and ordered 'to find caution for £3 to keep the peace for three months'. By 1877 *Fiery Cross* was a full-time excursion ship giving sailings to Elie in addition to her established services to North Berwick and Aberdour. Trips to view the new bridge at Dundee became popular, with two hours ashore. *Fiery Cross* reached the peak of her popularity in 1880, sailing to a wide variety of destinations including St Andrews. Special cruises were provided for events such as Kirkcaldy market, Inverkeithing's Lammas Fair, Alloa Fast Day and North Berwick flower show. On 14 September she sailed at 11 a.m. on a 'shooting excursion down the Forth, to the vicinity of the Bass Rock – parties will enjoy two or three hours shooting, and a boat will be lowered to pick up the birds'. *Fiery Cross* was known by a number of bynames including Auld Nonsuch, Granny's Washtub and Aiberdour Puddock – or to the thirsty as the 'Floatin' Shebeen'. Eclipsed by more modern vessels, *Fiery Cross*'s sailings reduced, but she was present at the opening of the Forth Bridge in 1890. Jamieson died in September 1893 and his little ship was broken up five years later. This picture shows *Fiery Cross* florrying at Aberdour, with *Lord Morton* just visible in the background approaching the wooden pier.

The Forth has a tidal range of up to twenty feet and all the early harbours dried out at low water. Only the new harbours at Granton, Burntisland and Leith, and the piers owned and operated by the Galloway Co. at Aberdour, Elie and North Berwick (the latter two described on page 16), could be approached at low water, making it necessary to ferry passengers ashore using what were locally known as 'florry boats'. These were in use until the 1920s, when the Queensferry piers were extended and the wooden pier at Aberdour reopened. These photographs are believed to show florry boats at May Island.

In 1874 *Lord Aberdour* became the property of John Kidd, a Leith wine merchant, and in 1876 he appointed Matthew Galloway (a Leith ship chandler and son of the vessel's former co-owner), as manager. Kidd introduced two new vessels that season, *Lord Elgin* and *Lord Mar*, and although intended specifically for the upriver traffic these also offered a twice-weekly service to Elie, with weekend cruises round the Bass Rock, as well as providing weekend assistance on the Aberdour passage. By 1878 *Lord Elgin* was entirely a firth cruise ship, running weekly to Dundee 'sailing alongside and under the longest bridge in the world'. *Lord Mar* was sold in March 1879, and thereafter firth sailings round the Bass Rock only operated on Saturdays. John Kidd died on 29 April 1880 and his executors sold *Lord Elgin* to Bournemouth operators in May 1881. This photograph shows her at Cowes on the Isle of Wight after conversion to a cargo steamer in 1921.

The Glasgow partnership of Matthew & Mathieson brought the eleven-year-old Clyde steamer *Carrick Castle* to the Forth, and she made her inaugural sailing on the queen's birthday, 19 May 1881, twice to the Bass Rock and with an evening trip to Aberdour. The *Scotsman* commented: 'In this fast mail boat, Elie could be reached in an hour, and Dundee in little over three'. Her adverts were subtitled 'The Swiftest on the East Coast'. Every Thursday she sailed round the Bass Rock, May Island and Bell Rock, and occasionally made trips down the Berwickshire coast to St Abb's Head. Upriver she ventured as far as Alloa, being based there during the local fair holidays. On Edinburgh holidays she ran to Aberdour. A similar programme applied for the next four seasons, with calls at Portobello wherever appropriate. She left the Forth on 2 May 1885 for the south of England. This photograph shows her reversing into a berth at the Broomielaw, Glasgow, with the steamer *Benmore* to her right. Only one very poor quality image is known to exist of her on the Forth.

The Forth River Steam Shipping Co. was formed in 1880, taking over *Lord Aberdour* and the low-water pier at Hawkcraig from John Kidd's executors. The company's manager was Matthew Galloway, and on 17 May 1880 he acquired a feu at Hawkcraig (Aberdour) at the entrance to the low-water pier, and had a large family house built there. Galloway became a daily commuter to Leith on his own steamer, and consequently when he was on board a call was always made at Hawkcraig Pier. The frequency of the Aberdour sailings was doubled in 1882 by chartering the tug *Livingstone*, judged a success as it 'induced a larger number of families to engage summer houses'. The Wallace brothers – Andrew, an Edinburgh solicitor, and John, a doctor in Liverpool – joined the partnership to finance an additional steamer called *Lord Morton*, built by S. & H. Morton of Leith for the Aberdour passage. Seen here when new, she attained thirteen knots on trials off Gullane on 23 April 1883, although with excess weight forward she steamed noticeably down at the bow. On her introduction the fare was reduced from 9*d*. to 6*d*., a rate which was maintained until 1914, even when sailings were made via Queensferry. Another similar but smaller steamer, *Stirling Castle*, was built specifically for the upriver trade in 1884.

Henderson & McKean operated tugs at Leith throughout the 1880s, using *Livingstone* and then *Gladstone* on a number of short-run excursions. Built as *Flying Meteor* in 1875 for the Clyde Shipping Co. by J. T. Eltringham of South Shields, *Gladstone* was typical of a fleet of near-identical tugs constructed for these owners over the next decade. A number of them subsequently came to the Forth: *Flying Owl* to Grangemouth as *Forth* in 1892; *Flying Bat* to Alloa in 1896; *Flying Fish* to Bo'ness in 1905; *Flying Swallow* to Kirkcaldy as *Fifeshire* in 1905; and *Flying Scotsman* as *Runner* to Grangemouth in 1912. In 1889 *Gladstone* was chartered to the Galloway Co. to supplement its Aberdour sailings, being sold to Dundee owners the following spring. She is seen here on arrival in Dundee, and was later renamed *Commodore*. Note the registration LH 1053, which allowed her to be used for fishing.

On 9 April 1886 the Forth River Steam Shipping Co. was dissolved and reconstituted as the Galloway Saloon Steam Packet Company (GSSP), with Thomas Aitken, of the London & Edinburgh Shipping Co., as chairman; Matthew Galloway as managing owner; and David Kidd and Andrew Wallace as directors. Capital was £32,000, but was soon increased by £12,000 (of which £8,450 was paid up). Robert Croall was the largest shareholder. *Edinburgh Castle*, a new steamer ordered by the previous partnership and built by J. Scott & Co. of Kinghorn, ran her trials on 8 May, achieving a speed of fifteen knots, and was placed on a new service between Leith and Largo. She had saloons the full width of the hull, giving increased internal comfort, and cooking was by steam from the main boiler, with a similar arrangement being used to keep dishes warm in the saloon bars. Electric lighting was fitted for use on evening cruises, and her single funnel was telescopic to allow her to pass under the Alloa Bridge. The new company's steamers were repainted in an attractive livery combining violet-grey hulls, varnished (later white) deck cabins, white paddleboxes and 'navy yellow' funnels. Smart new uniforms with the letter 'G' in gold braid on the yachting caps completed the makeover.

Lord Aberdour also received a telescopic funnel, as did the 1884-built *Stirling Castle*, which ran upriver. Here the former is seen at Aberdour, where she and *Lord Morton* were the regular vessels. The route of the Aberdour passage became triangular in 1886 when the Galloway Co. opened a long wooden pier at South Queensferry town harbour to accommodate the tourists flocking to see the Forth Bridge construction works.

Lord Morton seen at the stone pier at Aberdour in GSSP colours.

At the 1886 AGM of the GSSP, Thomas Aitken stated that the lack of low-water landing places presented the greatest obstacle to the operation of the excursion trade. The only locations where steamers could call regardless of tide were Leith, Portobello, Kirkcaldy, Aberdour and Alloa. At North Berwick a pier was built on the Platcock Rocks outside the harbour, and opened on 25 May 1888 when *Stirling Castle* took the town's provost and councillors on a luncheon cruise to Elie. A pier was required at Largo, but the foreshore lease was refused and the company provided a moving gangway instead. Again permission was refused and the gangway, a long eight-wheeled structure, was placed on Lundin beach, a mile east. Local opposition defeated a plan for a pier at this spot. At Elie, a pier on the rocks outside the harbour was opened in 1889 and modified with extra piling for the next season. Having provided a subsidy to Portobello Pier in 1889, the GSSP purchased it for £1,500 in June 1891. To operate to these new destinations, *Tantallon Castle*, seen here at the stone pier at Aberdour, was added to the fleet as its flagship, achieving fifteen knots on trial on 28 May 1887. 'The main saloon on deck . . . is upholstered in old gold plush, [and] is beautifully furnished in carved teak. Below is the dining saloon laid in crimson cloth, and seated for nearly 100 passengers. Electric light is supplied, 30 incandescent lights of 20 candlepower each illuminate the ship, and a bridge lamp is fitted to allow of the passengers landing with safety, on returning from the evening cruises.' All vessels were fitted with flying bridges for the 1887 season.

Tantallon Castle was built by S. & H. Morton of Leith and at 190 feet was the GSSP's largest steamer. Her boiler produced rather wet steam, however, and a much taller funnel was fitted after two or three seasons to increase the furnace draught. Down by the head like *Lord Morton*, she was lengthened by thirteen feet in 1895 to improve her trim, the extra portion being added behind the engine room. The problem of wet steam persisted and an auxiliary condenser was fitted in 1897 which increased engine revolutions by 5 per cent. Seen here at May Island *c.*1893, her cruises generally called at Elie and North Berwick en route to the Bell or Bass Rocks or May Island. Evening cruises round the Bass Rock, calling at Portobello or Kirkcaldy, featured most Fridays, while Sunday was the day for the long cruise, St Andrews being one of the most popular destinations, with Dundee, Berwick and even trips round the Farne Islands featuring occasionally.

Edinburgh Castle was found to be rather a lively sea boat, and after one season she and *Stirling Castle* (seen here) changed places, the latter becoming a firth cruise vessel. Also a product of S. & H. Morton's Leith yard, *Stirling Castle* had been built in 1884 for the upriver service. By 1888 she was giving many excursions from various coastal resorts to view the Forth Bridge, but a major role was acting as a feeder for *Tantallon Castle*, which would sail direct from Leith to Elie, while *Stirling Castle*, having called at Portobello and North Berwick, connected with her larger colleague there. She also served minor ports such as Kirkcaldy, Buckhaven, Methil, Largo and Dunbar. Behind the scenes, relations between the GSSP and the North British Railway were cool and on 1 July 1889 the railway sent a long letter complaining of interference with its rail traffic. Private negotiations followed and on 25 July Messrs Aitken, Croall, Galloway, Kidd and Watson sold 2,698 shares to nominee shareholders representing the North British Railway, giving the latter a 62.5 per cent holding in the GSSP. There was no outward sign of change, and the company continued to be managed from Leith with Aitken and Galloway at the helm.

In 1890 the fleet was commissioned early for the opening on 4 March of the Forth Bridge. The railway ferry *Thane of Fife* was chartered for the Edinburgh holiday on 22 May, and again in June, but by late July the much larger *John Stirling* was on charter to provide extra capacity for the Aberdour passage. She had too much draught and was slow, so tenders were requested for an additional ship, although in the event the NBR offered its newly reboilered Clyde steamer *Gareloch* at a price of £4,000, and after alterations at Leith she received a steam three certificate. Renamed *Wemyss Castle*, she was a smart looker, even if she didn't have deck saloons like the other vessels, and entered service in June 1891 on the Aberdour / Queensferry runs. Three steamers were now so employed, working triangularly, sailing direct to Aberdour in the mornings, while in the afternoon the route was reversed with runs from Aberdour direct. An 1896 innovation was the introduction of evening cruises landing at Pettycur, with the firth cruise ship also calling there on Mondays and Fridays in lieu of Portobello, where the pier was closed at weekends for repair. Following the effective takeover of the GSSP by the North British Railway, through booking facilities were made available from most Fife stations, with passengers joining the steamer at Elie.

The GSSP fleet's winter quarters were originally at Leith docks, but with the opening of the Forth Bridge two steamers were moved to Inverkeithing. For subsequent winters Aitken made arrangements with the Duke of Buccleuch to use Granton Quarry. Infilled long ago, this was situated near the present-day Gypsy Brae. In 1898 the fleet was laid up at Aberdour, behind the stone pier, but this proved unpopular with crews having to travel there by train from Leith. Instead, from 1899 Port Edgar became the winter base, remaining so until 1916. Here the fleet is seen in Granton Quarry (left to right): *Lord Aberdour, Tantallon Castle, Wemyss Castle, Lord Morton, Stirling Castle, Edinburgh Castle*. Note that the funnels are telescoped on those vessels so-fitted.

Stirling Castle backs out of Granton while acting as commodore ship for the Royal Forth Yacht Club's 1895 regatta. Heavy expenditure throughout the 1890s drained the company, with a major factor being continual repairs to Portobello Pier. On 20 September 1891 a new ballroom and tea room were swept into the sea, and the pier was then closed until May 1893. When it reopened local magistrates declined to grant a license for dancing, which was prohibited until 1896 when the pier was closed for weekend repairs after a minor accident involving *Tantallon Castle*. By 1897, for the first time in six years, it was considered safe. There was also heavy expenditure on *Tantallon Castle*, *Edinburgh Castle* and the elderly *Lord Aberdour*. All of the company's six ships were in service on 19 May 1898, the Edinburgh holiday, but four days later *Tantallon Castle* and *Stirling Castle* ran steaming trials and the following morning departed from the Forth, bound for Constantinople (now Istanbul), having been sold to Turkish owners for £13,150. Both ships were lost during the First World War.

The 1898 season was a shambles, commencing with *Wemyss Castle* (seen here at Elie) standing in as a firth cruise ship. Capacity was insufficient on the Aberdour run, so the Alloa tug *Flying Bat* was chartered and tiny *Lord Aberdour* hived off to Stirling to allow the larger *Edinburgh Castle* to assist. Then *Lord Morton* went off with boiler trouble, and finally *Wemyss Castle* was withdrawn with engine problems. Discontented passengers were rife, and the company's reputation took a hammering.

Replacement ships were ordered with the same names as their predecessors. *Tantallon Castle* (II) came from John Scott of Kinghorn and cost £15,686, while *Stirling Castle* (II) was ordered from the same builder at a cost of £11,791. At 210 feet the new *Tantallon Castle* (seen here off Leith) was the company's largest vessel to date. Her machinery gave her a speed of sixteen and a half knots, with accommodation for 787 passengers on a steam three certificate. Furnishings were lavish. The first class saloon was divided into three elliptical alcoves on each side, with walls panelled in oak, surmounted by an egg and dart cornice. The alcoves were separated by Grecian-style pilasters with capitals in walnut, inlaid with gold. The couches were upholstered in gold Utrecht velvet and there were stained glass windows at the aft end. *Tantallon Castle* (II) was launched with steam up on 6 May 1899, and entered service immediately.

With the firth cruises covered by the new flagship, *Flying Bat* was again chartered to assist at Aberdour, where both *Lord Morton* and *Wemyss Castle* were suffering from extreme boiler problems. All too often other steamers had to make for Aberdour to rescue stranded passengers, and to add to this *Tantallon Castle* (II) turned out to be a failure. In their anxiety to ensure that she was not bow-heavy like her predecessor, her builders erred too far in the opposite direction. She had insufficient weight forward and proved almost impossible to steer. On 28 June she collided with the Gibson steamer *Abbotsford* and was off service for ten days. Lifeboats were moved forward, and steady sails fitted, as shown here, but this had little effect and long cruises were abandoned. A new rudder was fitted in the autumn, but after two summers the company was glad to sell her when an offer of £15,259 was received from London in April 1901. Afterwards she had a series of owners and was never a success, ending her days in Portugal.

Stirling Castle leaving North Berwick. It was October 1899 before the new *Stirling Castle* was launched. She was 170 feet long, with similarly lavish internal fittings to her big sister. Her single funnel was telescopic, allowing her to work upriver, and her compound diagonal machinery disconnecting, with the main crank in two halves (port and starboard) allowing the single engine to effectively operate as two units when necessary, thus providing maximum manoeuvrability. She proved to be one of the most useful and versatile vessels the company ever possessed, and took up the role of firth cruise ship, being partnered with *Tantallon Castle* in 1900. Regular cruises sailed as far as the Carr lightship, and on Sundays she served Kirkcaldy and Methil, also running to the windings, although calls at the smaller ports of Largo, Anstruther and Dunbar were abandoned. The gangway at Lundin was moved to Aberdour and placed just east of the Hawkcraig Pier. It was used for low-water landings on Sundays, when the steamer tied up at the pier but florried her passengers to the gangway.

Lord Morton was reboiled for the 1900 season, lengthened by twelve feet immediately behind the engine room, and given fatter funnels. Costing £2,067, these alterations were carried out by Hawthorn's at Granton and eliminated her tendency to sail down by the head, making her a much better ship in all respects. By this time it was considered that two vessels could handle the Aberdour / Queensferry sailings, so *Lord Aberdour* was traded in as part payment for the work and broken up at Granton. This picture shows the West Pier at Leith, with the modified *Lord Morton* leaving and *Edinburgh Castle* moored.

Consideration was given to a replacement for *Tantallon Castle*, including the possibility of a turbine vessel. As it was felt that the delicate pier at Portobello couldn't stand the strain of such a ship, a triangular wooden extension was added to the structure in the winter of 1901–2, providing berths up- and downstream, and only connected to the iron pier by gangways. This work cost £2,152. 15s. 1d. Here *Stirling Castle* is moored below the ballroom, possibly in 1901 before the extension was added. To finance a new vessel, a share call was issued for the sum of £3,550, not previously paid up by shareholders (see page 14). The NBR share purchase of 1889 had left the Wallace brothers holding a 37.5 per cent interest, and very unhappy at the way the company was being managed; indeed after 1891 they had no further contact with it. Andrew and his late brother's executors refused to pay the share call, instead offering their shares for sale to the company. Their proposal was accepted, together with other minor holdings from directors. £16,180 was paid out, effectively reducing the company's capital from £43,160 to £26,980, and making the NBR sole owner but leaving no money for a new steamer. On 26 March 1903 the NBR board minuted its approval 'of the proposed dissolution of the co-partnership styled "The Galloway Saloon Steam Packet Company" '. However, when the GSSP board was called to ratify this decision on 29 July, Matthew Galloway presented the company's future prospects so eloquently that the decision was rescinded.

Despite this reprieve, the NBR proceeded to extract as much money as possible from the GSSP, and in April 1904 Galloway was told to lend £2,000 to the railway, followed by a further £8,000 the following month. The books of both concerns were adjusted to reflect this, but no money was transferred. In 1905, following the death of NBR director George Wieland, Thomas Aitken seized his chance and informed the board that *Wemyss Castle* would be unseaworthy by September, proposing to finance a twin screw ship from the company's depreciation fund. The railway board accepted this suggestion, and Aitken and Galloway used the money that should have been in the NBR's bank account to build *Roslin Castle*. Valuing £12,210. 12s. 11d., the order was placed with Hawthorn's of Leith in August; *Wemyss Castle* was sold for scrap for £475. Launched on 13 February 1906, *Roslin Castle* quickly became a popular ship with good looks, seaworthiness and a high standard of comfort. Measuring 185 feet, she was propelled by twin sets of triple expansion machinery.

Thomas Aitken died in February 1907 and was succeeded as chairman by a railway director, Henry Grierson. This marked the end of the GSSP's independence. An investigation of the accounts followed and the missing monies were identified, while at the same time it was deemed that the company should be contained within limits where it did not compete with the railway. The Stirling run was axed, and *Stirling Castle* (seen here at May Island) sold to Southampton owners (today's Red Funnel) for £8,750, the money being loaned to the NBR. Grierson also decreed that the steamers would carry no luggage, which would instead be sent in advance by rail, unless destined for the hotel and tea room adjacent to Hawkcraig Pier. Bulk purchasing was also arranged with the railway for coal and other common supplies.

In March 1908 the Admiralty was scouring the country for vessels to use as fleet tenders, and offered £15,000 for *Roslin Castle*. At 32 per cent over her building cost it was too good a price to turn down, and she became the fleet tender HMS *Nimble* (as illustrated here), surviving until 1949 when she was broken up in Belgium. There were no firth cruises in 1908 and the only pier down firth to receive calls was Methil, to which *Edinburgh Castle* sailed on Sundays. *Flying Bat* was again chartered for the trades week, running to Aberdour each weekend.

As a replacement for *Roslin Castle*, the company agreed to accept a Clyde steamer which the NBR stated would be surplus in 1909. This was *Redgauntlet*, and she arrived at Leith in March that year. Only her funnel livery was altered (to navy yellow – although the black top was retained), and she sailed with a black hull and varnished saloons. A transfer price of £4,000 was paid, and her electric lighting was improved and a steam windlass fitted. The cruise programme was more consistent than previously, and the following schedule, from 1909, is typical: via Portobello, Methil and Elie to the North Carr light or St Andrews (Monday); North Berwick and Bass Rock (Tuesday); North Berwick and May Island (Thursday and Friday); a double run to North Berwick and Bass Rock (Wednesday); a double run to Elie (Saturday); Methil and round Bass Rock (Sunday), the latter replaced by an upriver cruise from Methil in 1911. This picture shows *Redgauntlet* at Elie.

In January 1910 the board read a sombre report on the condition of *Redgauntlet*. The short, sharp seas of the firth had slackened her rivets to an alarming extent, and S. & H. Morton's tender for £1,150 was accepted for repairs, including the fitting of a small forecastle to stiffen the bow. A landing platform for use at May Island was built on this. Thereafter *Redgauntlet* (seen here at Methil) gave sterling service.

Latterly *Redgauntlet* received a new funnel, without the ring which had divided the red and white portions when she was painted in NBR colours. This photograph was taken at North Berwick.

The livery worn by *Redgauntlet* proved so much less expensive to maintain that it was applied to the other two steamers. By 1910 *Lord Morton*'s funnels had black tops, and her saloons were varnished in dark brown. This view shows her leaving Leith with the Grangemouth-registered tug *Blücher* at the West Pier.

THE WEST PIER, LEITH.

Lord Morton's hull had been painted black by 1911, though white paddle boxes were retained. This picture shows her at the West Pier, Leith. At the close of the 1912 season the GSSP reported its highest passenger receipts for many years, and money was released to the railway by reducing the capital by £20,000; the company was now a positive asset on the NBR's balance sheet. John Galloway succeeded his father as manager on the latter's death on 10 November 1913, aged 70. Henry Grierson died on 26 January 1914, Bruce Gilroy being appointed chairman.

West Pier, Leith.

Calls at Kirkcaldy were resumed in 1913, with *Flying Bat* being based there and providing a service to Inchkeith, the Forth Bridge and Portobello. In 1914 both *Flying Bat* and *Forth* were chartered to maintain the Aberdour service while the GSSP's own steamers undertook charter sailings, many originating from the river ports of Bo'ness and Grangemouth. Tugs had previously catered for most of this traffic, but the Board of Trade had increased safety requirements following the *Titanic* disaster in 1912 and as a result many tugs had their passenger certificates cancelled. John Wilson's Bo'ness fleet was particularly badly affected. By this time *Edinburgh Castle* had also received a new funnel, no longer telescopic, and she is very smartly turned out in this picture showing her backing out of Kirkcaldy harbour.

In February 1914 the GSSP considered purchasing the Dundee-based *Slieve Bearnagh* but the NBR objected. Instead her owners, D. & J. Nicol of Dundee, brought her to the Forth, and on 8–10 July 1914 she sailed between Kirkcaldy and Leith, returning after the Dundee holidays. From 1 August she was sailing daily from Kirkcaldy and Leith round the Bass Rock. On renewing its pier lease at Hawkcraig, the GSSP had a clause inserted that no rights would be granted to competitors, preventing *Slieve Bearnagh* and others from calling there.

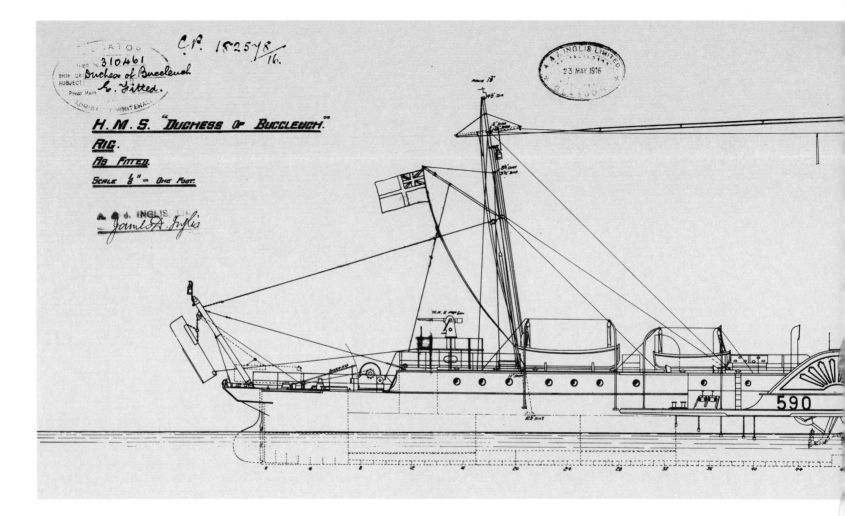

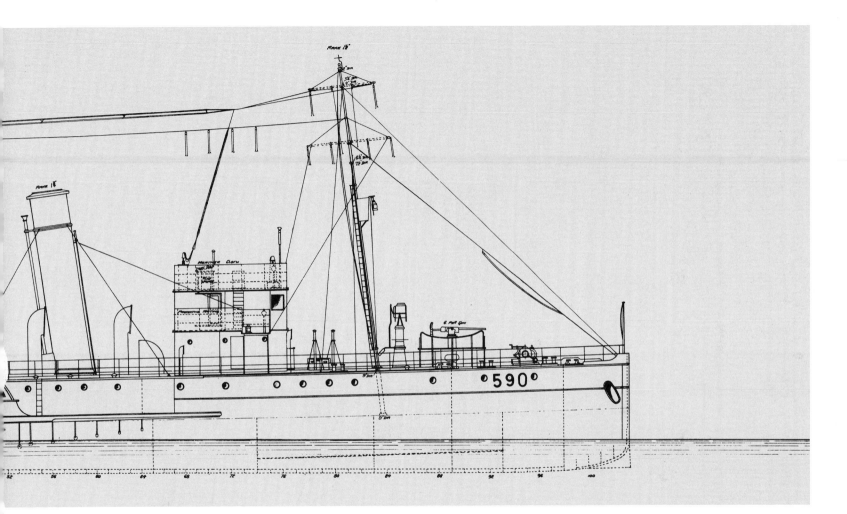

In October 1914, even though war had already been declared with Germany, the NBR entered into negotiations with Glasgow shipbuilders A. & J. Inglis for two new steamers, one for the Clyde and the other for the Forth. Delivery of the Forth ship, at a cost of £27,500, was promised for May 1915. At 225 feet long she would have been the finest ever vessel to sail on the Forth. Named *Duchess of Buccleuch*, she was purchased by the Admiralty and completed as a minesweeper in April 1916, the company receiving £3,550 compensation. Laid up at Llanelli, in Wales, after the war, she was broken up there in 1921. This rigging plan carries stamps by both the builders and the Admiralty, and is signed by Dr Inglis.

At the start of the First World War *Slieve Bearnagh* returned to Dundee and the Galloway fleet was laid up at Port Edgar. *Redgauntlet* departed for minesweeping duties on 23 May 1915, the other ships moving to Bo'ness when the Admiralty took over Port Edgar as a minesweeping base. They too were requisitioned on 28 June, and after much haggling the Admiralty purchased the three ships on 12 August 1917. After the war, *Redgauntlet* (seen here as a minesweeper) was sold to French interests in Algeria. In 1919, along with *Slieve Bearnagh*, *Lord Morton* and *Edinburgh Castle* formed part of a British and American expeditionary force sent to Russia to support the fight against the Bolsheviks. The two Forth steamers were blown up by British forces in the White Sea to avoid capture on 24 September 1919. *Slieve Bearnagh* survived, only to be laid up at Inverkeithing until scrapped there. By April 1915 a military billet had been established on Portobello Pier, but late in 1917 the pier was declared unsafe. On 17 January the following year the GSSP accepted an offer to demolish it for £2,180, and it came down that spring. By the end of the war the company's assets were piers at Hawkcraig, North Berwick, Elie and South Queensferry, ticket boxes at Methil and Elie, and a florry boat at Aberdour. The pier leases were cancelled in February 1921, the Earl of Morton being paid £1,200 in lieu of repairs at Hawkcraig. The company then went into liquidation.

After the First World War the Grangemouth & Forth Towing Co. initially had a monopoly on Forth cruises. In 1920 the Victoria Jetty at Leith was the departure point, reverting to the more usual West Pier the following year. There was a programme almost daily from 1 July 1920 to Aberdour, Kirkcaldy and the Forth Bridge, mostly provided by *Runner* (seen here at Aberdour), with some assistance from *Forth*, both of which were former Clyde tugs. *Forth* was withdrawn after the 1923 season and *Runner* early in 1927. In 1926 cruising was limited to weekends and the trades holiday by the general strike. Small privately owned motor launches appeared, with *Barnbogle Castle* cruising from Cramond for a few years from 1922. Other launches operated from the beach at Portobello (the first was *Lion* in 1923) for trips round the bay, and from Aberdour to Inchcolm, from North Berwick round the Bass Rock (*St Baldred's*), and from Anstruther to the May Island.

THE STONE PIER, ABERDOUR.

West Pier, Leith Docks

A new company, Kirk, Deas & Co., introduced the large salvage tug *Conqueror* in 1922. Dating from 1887, she was 131 feet long and is seen here at the West Pier, Leith. Advertised as the ship with two yellow funnels, she possessed a steam three certificate and commenced a programme of morning cruises to the Forth Bridge and elsewhere, afternoon cruises to Aberlady or Largo (sometimes via Aberdour or Kirkcaldy), and evening cruises, again to the Forth Bridge. Calls at Kirkcaldy were frequent. Occasionally, full-day cruises were offered and use was made of the old Galloway pier at Elie.

For the 1924 season, by which time she was owned by the Stanley–Butler Steamship Co. of Kirkcaldy, *Conqueror* sported black-topped red funnels and a grey hull. A point was made of landing somewhere on the cruises, with Dysart being a frequent port of call, while at weekends the regular route was from Kirkcaldy via Leith to Blackness, where arrangements were made with the Ministry of Works to call at the castle pier. Elie was also featured, and *Conqueror* was the final vessel to call at the Galloway pier there. For 1925 the company obtained the lease of the repaired Hawkcraig Pier at Aberdour. By this stage *Conqueror* belonged to Teesside owners, who renamed her *Hurworth* and chartered her to the Kirkcaldy operators, for whom she operated on a steam four certificate on a reopened Aberdour passage.

For the 1926 season the Stanley–Butler Steamship Co. obtained the pretty *Princess of Wales* on deferred payment terms from the New Medway Steam Packet Co. Dating from 1896, she was 140 feet long and of raised quarterdeck design. For the next two years she maintained the Aberdour passage with cruises to the Forth Bridge. Sailings were severely restricted in 1926 by the coal strike, and in March 1927 she sank at her moorings in Kirkcaldy harbour. Having been salvaged, she opened the service on 4 June but broke down and was off service for a week. With increased competition from the Grangemouth & Forth Towing Co. the company was unable to maintain its payments to New Medway, which foreclosed at the end of the season and forced the Kirkcaldy partnership into liquidation. Seen here on the Medway before coming to the Forth, *Princess of Wales* was scrapped the following year.

The Grangemouth & Forth Towing Co. replaced its passenger tug *Runner* with a proper excursion steamer for 1927. This was *Fair Maid*, dating from 1886, measuring 190 feet long and well-known on Clyde sailings as *Isle of Skye*. She opened the cruise season from Leith on 5 June, offering 'music and dancing on board, teas and light refreshments at shore prices'. *Fair Maid* gave a simple programme of excursions to Aberdour (using florry boats until 1929 when approval to call at Hawkcraig was obtained) and Kirkcaldy, with frequent bridge cruises. Generally there were three departures daily from Leith at about 11.30, 2.30 and 6.30. Return fares were 2s. cabin and 1s. 6d. steerage. There were also a number of public charters, some of which sailed upriver as far as Alloa. From 1934 the Kirkcaldy calls were confined to twice-weekly and the Aberdour calls increased, with cruises added to Blackness Castle, Rosyth or round the Three Inches (Inchmickry, Inchcolm and Inchgarvie). This picture shows *Fair Maid* at Leith, still in her Clyde livery with white funnel.

For her excursion programme *Fair Maid* operated from the West Pier, where this photograph was taken. She continued in service until 28 August 1939 when Admiralty regulations on the movement of vessels in the Firth of Forth were issued. In November 1940 she was requisitioned for duty as an Admiralty tender based at Craigendoran on the Clyde, going to the breakers' yard in 1945.

In 1934–6 competition was provided by the Redcliffe Shipping Co. of Hull, for whom George A. Morrison & Co. acted as local agents. Built at Dundee in 1903 for ferry service on the Humber and originally called *Cleethorpes*, *Cruising Queen* commenced services on 9 June 1934, operating from the West Pier, Leith, on non-landing afternoon cruises to North Berwick, Elie Ness or towards Grangemouth. Evening cruises to Blackness or round the Three Inches followed. *Cruising Queen* provided the first open firth cruises in ten years, but was rather slow and found difficulty in getting back to Leith in time for her evening trip. Fares were 2*s*. for the afternoon cruise and 1*s*. 6*d*. for the evening cruise. On excursions to Aberdour or Kirkcaldy tickets cost 1*s*. 3*d*. single or 2*s*. return.

Realising *Cruising Queen*'s limitations, the company purchased the former MacBrayne passenger and mail steamer *Fusilier*, which was lying at Ardrossan having been replaced by a new motor vessel. Her Forth season commenced on 4 August 1934 sailing from Granton (where she was based, and where this photograph was taken) for Largo, followed by an upriver evening cruise. She dated from 1888 and was 202 feet long, with a clipper bow, figurehead and bowsprit. Frequent calls were made at Kirkcaldy during the following six weeks on cruises to the Bass Rock, May Island, Anstruther or the Forth Bridge. *Fusilier* proved a wet ship when steaming into the short seas in the firth, and no passengers were allowed on deck forward of the saloon. She was also extravagant on fuel. On 2 September *Cruising Queen* finished her season and sailed south to Hull on 25 September. She went to the breakers' yard during the winter. *Fusilier* continued until 17 September, her final runs being to view the Atlantic fleet lying at anchor east of the Forth Bridge. She was sold to Welsh owners over the winter.

Another former Humber ferry replaced both *Cruising Queen* and *Fusilier*. This was *Brocklesby*, dating from 1912 and renamed *Highland Queen* for her Forth service. She was 195 feet long, double-ended, with rudders at each end, and certificated to carry 750 passengers. Because her paddles were in such a poor state she was restricted to ten knots. Cruises commenced from Leith on 4 May 1935, with trips to the Bass Rock, the Forth Bridge and Rosyth. She sailed daily at 2.30 and 7.30, with a special late cruise on Saturdays leaving about 10.15 p.m. just after the pubs closed. Her engines were run at half speed on this cruise! Though advertised to sail round the Bass, her lack of speed often meant that she had to turn off North Berwick. For the 1936 season she was based at Granton, where even using both rudders she had difficulty entering and leaving the harbour. Only one boiler was lit, as an economy move, and on more that one occasion she had to stop while an engineer climbed into the paddle box to carry out repairs. She did not proceed further downriver than Fidra, and as it was thought that better traffic might be had at Lowestoft she sailed there from Granton on 29 July 1936, being sent to a shipbreaker's at the end of the year.

John Hall (Cruises) Ltd. was formed early in 1947 by a successful Kirkcaldy baker of the same name. The former Scarborough vessel *New Royal Lady* was purchased, still painted in Admiralty grey, and refitted by Menzies of Leith. Having been renamed *Royal Lady* she entered service on 1 May 1947. Built for coastal cruising in 1938, she was 137 feet long and was based at Granton, though some cruises commenced at Burntisland, which appeared as a cruise port for the first time, being no longer restricted by the exclusive rights of a parliamentary ferry. Emphasis was laid on the carnival atmosphere on board and at 7s. 6d. fares were high, being reduced on 1 June to 4s. (5s. on Wednesdays, Saturdays and Sundays) when recordings replaced a live band. *Royal Lady* was then sold at a profit to General Steam Navigation for service on the Medway as *Crested Eagle*, and left the Forth in early October. Having been renamed *Imperial Eagle*, she operated between Malta and Gozo from 1957.

For the 1948 season Hall went on to purchase two 112-foot ex-naval launches, which he converted for passenger use and re-engined with American diesels, giving a speed of twelve knots. It was his intention to use one on the Forth and the other on the Tay, and they were named *Royal Forth Lady* and *Royal Tay Lady*, though the 'Royal' prefix was dropped after a complaint from the Lord Lyon. *Forth Lady* revived the Inchcolm service from a base at Granton, also giving evening trips to the Forth Bridge. In late August she was relieved by *Tay Lady* until the season ended on 20 September. Over the winter the Tay vessel (seen here at Perth) was renamed *Ulster Lady* and sent to Belfast. In 1951 she sailed on the Clyde, and then returned to the Forth for use on the revived Burntisland ferry.

Forth Lady's certificate was for 170 passengers, and she was fitted with a 70-seat bar and 50-seat tea lounge, both upholstered in leatherette and moquette and lit by strip lighting, then a novelty. Under the ownership of Forth Ferries Ltd., she continued the Inchcolm service from August 1950. The following year the new Burntisland ferry blocked her Granton berth and the Inchcolm run was suspended, with the result that she was laid up at Leith until being sold in 1954 for conversion into a yacht. The Granton–Inchcolm service reopened as part of an Edinburgh city coach tour from 1961 to 1964, operated by the Queensferry-based vessel *The Second Snark*. This picture shows *Forth Lady* at Inchcolm.

Three privately owned launches, *Victory*, *Skylark* and *Starcrest*, were based at Burntisland by the 1950s. These vessels operated off mobile gangways on beaches, running from Aberdour to Inchcolm, as well as providing 'Round the Bay' cruises from Portobello beach, as *Victory* is doing here. She had been built in 1922 as *May Queen* for service at Rothesay and came to the Forth in 1949. After being laid up following the death of her owner, she was purchased in 1981 by John Watson of South Queensferry, who renamed her *Maid of the Forth* and restarted the Inchcolm service from Queensferry. She was replaced by a larger vessel the following year. *Skylark* went to Loch Lomond about 1970 and still operates out of Balloch. Also in use at Portobello in the late 1940s were two ex-American army amphibious personnel carriers (DUKWs), which loaded passengers off the sands for short trips round the bay.

Starcrest at Inchcolm.

From September 1977 until December 1998 treated Lothian sewage was dumped beyond May Island or ten miles off St Abb's Head. The sludge ship *Gardyloo* was built by James Lamont & Co. of Port Glasgow and operated from a berth in Imperial Dock, Leith, where she is seen here. Group bookings of twelve passengers were taken on the vessel's daily run, offering what was a very attractive free cruise. Following EU legislation banning dumping at sea, she was sold in 1999 to Unibos Shipping Corporation and resold to Whittaker Tanker Company later that year. In 2004 she was still in service.

In 1997 Jim Reaper of Anstruther purchased the 100-seater *Dart Princess* from Torquay owners. Having been renamed *May Princess*, she replaced the launches *Sapphire II* and *Serenity* on landing excursions from Anstruther to the May Island, offering two to three hours ashore. Earlier launches on this service included the fishing vessel *Bright Reward* (1980), followed by *Sapphire I*. An open launch, *Sula II*, the second of the name, is owned by A. W. Mann and cruises from North Berwick harbour round the Bass Rock. *Sula II* can carry 71 passengers. This photograph shows *May Princess* at Anstruther.

The preserved paddle steamer *Waverley* visited the Forth in 1981, 1982 and 1983, calling at Granton and Burntisland on cruises. More recently, however, it has been her running mate, the 1949 *Balmoral*, which has made the Forth visits, usually for a few days in spring. This photograph shows her at Aberdour in 1989 on her first visit. There have been no further calls here, but she visited the Forth for a few days on journeys round Britain in 1990, 1993–5, 1997 and 1998–2002. Cruises took place from Granton, Burntisland and Anstruther to May Island, Bass Rock, Eyemouth and Berwick-on-Tweed. One-way trips have been offered to Amble and Newcastle, returning by coach. Leith was substituted for Granton in 2000, and Rosyth for Burntisland the following year.

Operating on the Queensferry–Inchcolm service for which she was built in 1988, *Maid of the Forth* (III) also offers jazz evening cruises, and from 2002 has run these from a variety of departure points including Port Seton, Fisherrow, Newhaven and St David's, where she is seen here in August 2003. She has also run from North Berwick for the Royal Society for the Protection of Birds. Some of her 2004 Inchcolm sailings are scheduled to operate from Newhaven.